THE METAVERSE

EXPLORE ALL THE SECRETS OF THE METAVERSE, LEARN HOW TO MOVE IN THIS NEW WORLD, AND TAKE A DEEP LOOK INTO THE FUTURE

MARTIN CROSS

TABLE OF CONTENTS

INTRODUCTION

Metaverse is a collection of various virtual worlds, game worlds if you want, capable of possible cooperation. This means that these worlds and the games they are represented in them will be connected at some point in the future. But it doesn't stop with the games. In the Metaverse, you can virtually check an NFT gallery of famous real-world artists, play a game on your mobile while your friends play the same game from XBOX or PS5, you can then check a new musical artist in his recent virtual streamed performance, and finally to perform almost every programmable simulation of a situation from our lives, such as learning to drive a car, plane, a rocketship, and so one.

This book is a definitive guide into this novel technology called Metaverse. The content within these pages covers all you need to comprehend this remarkable concept fully.

Facebook, Epic Games, Microsoft, and the blockchain-related world are all betting on the digital universe in which we tend and will tend to spend more and more time.

But the Metaverse doesn't just offer entertainment opportunities; it offers great profit opportunities. From the point of view of technological jargon, 2021 has been particularly rich in neologisms: from DeFi (decentralized finance based on blockchain) to GameFi (allowing to earn money through video games); from the explosion of NFT to the sci-fi promises of the Metaverse. Finance, art, work, entertainment: in the second year marked by the coronavirus, the digital innovation sector has shown (not by chance) a willingness to move an increasingly large part of our lives online.

The Metaverse is an online space that allows you to interact more in an intensive way, so while you are on your VR headsets, you can create an avatar to represent you. You can walk around, go to school, night clubs and even interact with other people in the world. Advocates of the Metaverse see it as the next big thing. The Chief executive officer of Facebook, Mark Zuckerberg, says Facebook will transition from a social media platform to a Metaverse platform in the next five years. The company has moved to invest heavily in its virtual reality headsets and glasses, which will ultimately create lots of jobs for people. Other investors and companies are interested, and they want to be a part of this next big thing.

The beauty of how the Metaverse works is that what plays out before you completely depends on you. The features you will be exploring will largely depend on what tickles your fancy. It could be a digital salon, meeting, conference, or your favorite hangout. The first step is to join, and you'll be able to experience your desires. The Metaverse will be a community with an economy. You'll own your space, and by using an online Avatar, you will be able to move, speak, interact and collaborate with others.

Metaverse works in such a way that you'll have access to complete autonomy where you can both own and rent out virtual lands and properties just like you would own and rent out physical lands and properties. Another interesting feature is the creation of arts and buildings, which you could decide to sell to other Metaverse users by using non-fungible tokens (NFTs) or some other measures of values.

METAVERSE FUNDAMENTALS

CHAPTER 1: WHAT THE METAVERSE IS

The Metaverse is a shared virtual 3D world that provides an online world for interaction, immersion, and collaboration among users. Metaverse also is a virtual world where you can buy and sell virtual land, avatars, names, engage in virtual property rent, and best Metaverse investment stocks. These transactions are often done using cryptocurrency.

The Metaverse has also been referred to as the internet brought to life or at least rendered in 3D. It's a virtual environment of endless connectivity where people can attend events, hang out with friends, organize meetings, conferences, go shopping, etc., using virtual reality headsets and augmented reality glasses. This can be explored on smartphone apps or other devices.

To establish a connection with the Metaverse, one will almost certainly require the usage of a device. These goggles, a camera-equipped head-mounted gadget, or other innovative inventions are all possibilities. While they aren't required to participate in the Metaverse, these gadgets may undoubtedly enhance the experience. Users will interact with virtual items in real life by "wearing" a device that integrates all of its components.

To put this idea into practice, imagine waking up every day, donning your Metaverse goggles, and entering the Metaverse.

Think this is all just science fiction? No, not at all.

The Google Glass goggles were initially designed to be used for this purpose. You'll be able to observe and interact with virtual information as you walk down the street.

There is a possibility that you are walking to the railway station, and a virtual notification informs you of significant train delays. After that, you have the option of using a quicker route, such as public transportation or carpooling.

This is just a tentative example of how the Metaverse can work in real life. And if you still doubt it is happening, think again. The revolution has already begun.

Virtual items are presented in front of you, in the actual world, in real-time, and you can interact with them. Think of yourself as Tony Stark.

Using your artificial intelligence (AI) helper, you'll be able to find and see the information you're looking for in the actual world virtually. You can then view, click on, or otherwise interact with the things that appear.

Mobile technology has already made it possible for people to live in an enhanced reality, unnerving as it may sound. Your device is aware of your location and time. Since the Internet was created, integrating the real world with the virtual world has been an ongoing process. The Metaverse's primary function is to provide a means of distancing oneself from the realities of the real world. Adventures and alternate lives are possible in Fortnite for those who wish to do so. This escapist worldview has seen a substantial transformation in recent years with the inclusion of real-life components. Is watching a movie on Roblox something you'd like to do? You're playing Grand Theft Auto, and you'd want to buy some sneakers. On TikTok, you may watch a K-pop band's most recent live performance. As trade and engagement move online and into virtual worlds, the Metaverse is fueled by this virtual and real-life convergence. What are the commercial uses of the Metaverse, and who will reap the benefits? To put it another way, the introduction of the Metaverse will change our lives forever. Every industry has potential for Metaverse applications.

The possibilities the Metaverse will unlock are endless, from consumer-driven ones like retail to manufacturing and construction and beyond.

It is possible to make purchases in a flash. You won't even have to touch your smartphone to see a product when you see it in a store or on the Metaverse. Through a single account, customers may buy products and compare pricing. Due to improved connectivity, businesses will sell their products anywhere globally, regardless of where their retail locations may be.

Thanks to this new technology, businesses and celebrities will reach a far broader audience and collaborate more easily. In the future, customers will be able to communicate directly with brands. If employed correctly, this could have an excellent commercial influence. Brands and celebrities will see an increase in exposure. There may even be a market for virtual real estate in the Metaverse. Non-fungible tokens and other digital products and property will be given more attention in the future (NFTs). Because they aren't subject to wear and tear, items that can be traded are more valuable. Players may look forward to more immersive and interconnected game worlds in the future. A skin or item acquired in one game can be utilized in another game or swapped for a different item. As virtual cinema allows for private viewings with friends, the social experience will also shift. Many businesses, including journalism, social media, technology, and retail, will find new monetizing methods. At the same time, people will meet, work, and socialize more agreeably online in the future. Intellectual property will play a significant role when it comes to creative activity. Because of its greater accessibility, information, products, entertainment, and social experiences are likely to benefit consumers the most from the Metaverse. The technology market will be dominated by hardware and software enterprises. Providing hardware and software for the Metaverse is expected to rise significantly. Businesses will be able to build their virtual worlds. This means that more people will see and hear about brands and celebrities. As technology improves, so will the potential to provide customers with more relevant commercial offerings and experiences.

Law and rules in the Metaverse are still in flux. Therefore, legal guidance will also be required. As the virtual and real worlds merge, there is a tremendous demand for assistance in data protection, privacy, advertising rules, and ensuring that commercial firm intellectual property assets are secured. For years to come, attorneys and legislators will face the issue of making sure that real-world laws are appropriately translated into the virtual world. The Metaverse is being built by whom? The gaming industry is one of the best examples of how the Metaverse can be used in business today. We can see how the Metaverse can transform the way people interact with digital and real worlds through games like Fortnite and Roblox. As a result, many of the gaming industry's biggest names are also at the forefront of technological innovation and growth in this sector. Take the game Roblox, for instance. The gaming firm, which went public in March 2021, partially laid out its ambition for the company and the adoption of the Metaverse in its prospectus. For Roblox, a pervasive human co-experience platform is the aim, as computing power, high-bandwidth Internet connections, and human interface technologies continue to increase (and even build an economy based on its currency, Robux). Second Life's founders, Linden Labs, also developed their currency and had a bigger GDP than some small countries at one point.

In this situation, user experience is only one factor. Using the prefix "meta" (meaning beyond) and the stem "verse," the word "Metaverse" is formed (meaning the universe). Critics believe that several critical features must exist for the Metaverse to fulfill its full potential, including:

- Persistence
- The ability to give live, synchronous experiences
- Interoperability
- Value creation

Many stakeholders (individuals, commercial companies, and governments) are expected to be involved in the creation and operation of the Metaverse. This makes sense. Developing a community of stakeholders in the Metaverse, like the current Internet, is necessary for new technologies, businesses, services, content creators, standards and protocols, legislation, and more.

Microsoft's HoloLens augmented reality headset and Facebook's recent purchase of Oculus VR, as well as Unity's significant investment in digital twin technology, all point to the fact that many of the current technology industry giants, such as Microsoft, Facebook, and Unity, will almost certainly play a significant role in the development of the Metaverse.

In the future of the Metaverse, there's no consensus on how it will work, who will develop it, or who will "own" it (if anyone).

However, the broad consensus is that it will exist and no longer be considered a figment of our imaginations.

No matter what happens in the future, one thing is clear: The Metaverse will expand incrementally over time as capabilities evolve and synergies are formed.

CHAPTER 2: PRELIMINARY ELEMENTS AND TOOLS TO BE MASTERED TO START EVEN IF YOU ARE A NEWBIE

Metaverse's Key Characteristics

The Metaverse Is Endless

The Metaverse is a continuation of what we consider to be real. Since it is not bound by the physical world of the universe wherein we function, it can be said to transcend to infinity. The Metaverse has no boundaries.

A Synchronous Metaverse Is One in Which Everything Happens at the Same Time

It also provides simultaneous communication between users from all over the world, which is an important feature to mention. As a result, it enables trillions potentially of individuals to interact in real-time.

A Thriving Economy Exists in the Metaverse

This statement goes hand in hand with the first essential element mentioned before. Users can offer and receive the same experiences as they would in the actual world because it is an extension of the real world. Artists, for example, can conduct art displays, philosophers can hold talks, coworkers can hold meetings, and the list goes on. A basic token mechanism can be utilized to trade value.

Interoperability Is a Feature of a Metaverse

This is an understandably divisive topic to bring up. How can we define interoperability if we declare the Metaverse is only an extension of our own reality? And if interoperability is required, then must mean that numerous different Metaverses exist in silos, right?

This is correct. However, when we say the Metaverse is interoperable, we imply that whatever skin I chose for my character in one notion of the Metaverse can be easily transferred to another conception being implemented by a separate company.

Many entities have the power to create their own Metaverse, which must be remembered.

Meta, for example, might build a social place for its users, or Microsoft could develop a specific co-working Metaverse. The core idea is the same, but the execution is different.

Fundamentals Of The Metaverse

The Metaverse is a collection of virtual environments where you may collaborate and create with individuals who are not physically there with you. You will be able to engage with your friends, work, play, explore, shop, and create, among other things. Metaverse is not about putting in more time online; it is about making the time you put in more worthwhile. Fortunately for businesses, the Metaverse is not a single product that a single company can develop. The Metaverse, similar to the internet, exists whether or not Meta is involved. Therefore, different businesses' creations and ideas will work together. Let's have a tour around the various levels and components of this virtual environment, as well as the firms competing with each other and the larger firms' acquisitions and investments.

Data Requirement

The Metaverse is deeply rooted in our location. Our experience is shaped by where we are in the universe, not just regarding GPS location but also by our immediate surroundings, whether outside or inside. What room are we in, and who or what things or persons are in our immediate vicinity? What virtual avatars, creatures, information layers, or interactive elements can we find?

Ethics in the Metaverse

A major source of worry in the Metaverse is how to prevent toxicity or poor conduct in which people harass or intimidate others. Because many will be in the Metaverse, it is obligatory upon its builders to make it a safe area for everybody. For example, people's opinions about sexuality might alter throughout time.

The difficulty had also evolved since, when we initially began with these internet experiences, whether virtualized or not, they did not incorporate as much of the actual world as they do now. The situation has changed. The

Metaverse will soon be a lot more like being in the actual world. There are issues we have to go through that no one else has gone through.

People will act if they see the Metaverse as an add-on to reality rather than reality itself. Non-player characters may become more realistic, or perhaps smarter, in the future. According to Bartle, they may exhibit self-awareness. This might happen in the next few years, and it will take quantum computing to accomplish.

This poses a slew of ethical concerns. Are you going to eliminate the AI folks by erasing the database or turning it off? You might be able to resurrect them or at least duplicate them. Or do you destroy them by duplicating them? Have you become a mass killer if you develop a virtual environment for the sole purpose of killing characters?

You will then select the universe you want to visit, which might be social or gaming realms. We will see a slew of small worlds or Metaverses. A translation mechanism might be used to transport objects across Metaverse worlds.

You have to respect your players. Because you cannot leave the actual world if you do not like it, you will not be able to travel to another world where you do not have white hair. You have no choice but to remain in this reality. However, reality necessitates competition. You can always "go" to someone else's world if world operators surround you. You will have to respect them, or they will end up playing for someone else.

Simply, players want a place where they can be happy and be their best versions. In the physical world, the dice roll defines you. You do not have to be yourself in the virtual environment. You can uncover who you truly are. That is the kind of thing you would like to be able to see in the future.

Protocol Requirement Solution

With so many possibilities in the Metaverse, it is no surprise that so many technological behemoths continue to spend substantially on its growth. Because of the enormous potential influence, many people feel that this will be the next large-scale technology after the internet.

However, creating the "next internet" is easier said than done. Technical support for multiple dimensions and purposes, such as the ideal business economy, payment system, website economy, and other Web 3.0 aspects, is necessary to create the Metaverse.

As a Polkadot-based cross-chain protocol, X Protocol intends to fill this need. Polkadot (DOT) is a system that enables multiple blockchains to communicate in a similar way to the traditional internet by connecting different networks using Wanchain's decentralized bridges, a blockchain network interoperability framework. X Protocol thinks that by utilizing these elements, they will realize their goal of creating a "decentralized Metaverse based on Web 3.0."

To enter the Metaverse, the X Protocol leverages Web 3.0. The protocol will establish a fair and decentralized standard for all economic activity while ensuring that any firm can freely distribute content. As a result, users may compare the X Protocol public chain to Ethereum (ETH), a blockchain well-known for its smart contract capabilities.

According to X Protocol, the focus has shifted to the basic layer one infrastructure, which comprises source-generated games and lands models. The project is written in RUST and revolves around the Polkadot and Solana (SOL) environment, comprising the protocol and application layers. The layers' major goals are to get organic traffic in the Metaverse using self-developed decentralized apps (DApps) and give third-party DApps zero-barrier access to technological solutions.

X Protocol intends to produce DApps to attract organic users, then incorporate each DApp via Metaverse scenarios and give third-party DApps easy access to them; this will eventually result in a Metaverse environment with a huge number of participants and use cases. On Polkadot and Solana, X Protocol is rated one of the top Metaverse projects in a group experience, linked wallets, and GitHub code volume.

On the X Protocol, a DeFi cross-chain asset pool is being constructed so that tokens generated on many blockchains may be freely exchanged irrespective of which chain they originate from. The X cross-chain bridge may be used to implement this swap capability on the platform. The X Protocol team believes that their approach will "significantly lower the transaction barrier" and "enhance the trading experience for users."

Innovations Towards Building Mobile Gaming

It is difficult to move around the gaming industry without encountering someone who is discussing the Metaverse. Suppose you are unfamiliar with the Metaverse idea in games; the most basic explanation is that it is a linked world of virtual environments, similar to what Ernest Cline imagined in his cult novel Ready Player One, which has since been vividly brought to life as a Steven Spielberg movie.

Epic Games launched a $1 billion investment for these linked virtual environments, including $200 million from Sony, bringing the Metaverse one step closer to life. According to Epic CEO Tim Sweeney, the Metaverse will be constructed through open standards to connect various experiences.

The Metaverse is still in its early development, but in the meanwhile, we can see some positive signs and what it might look like in the mobile gaming industry. Therefore, let us look at what features of mobile games are expected to change for the Metaverse to come to life.

Immersion

It's not yet clear how deep one will go into the Metaverse. According to the Oasis in Ready Player One, it's like a haptic whole-body suit with virtual reality spectacles. On the plus side, we see tremendous advancements in virtual reality technology. Oculus moves away from bulky, Computer-reliant headgear with external tracking and toward more affordable standalone gadgets like the Quest 2 with internal tracking.

Yet, the future of virtual reality appears to be firmly anchored in console, PC, or standalone headsets like the Quest. While augmented reality is the dominating reality on smartphones, smartphones and virtual reality have yet to come together. The rumor mill has gone crazy about creating "Apple Glass" augmented reality technology, but who knows?

Full-body tracking will be required in the Metaverse as well. Some innovative advances, like the technology designed in collaboration with the Axis XR Interface system for the newly unveiled Virtual Taekwondo Olympic events, transform the whole body into a controller.

Content Delivery Infrastructure

The smartphone world is almost entirely reliant on Apple and Google for content distribution. Individuals must first download an application, after which they can choose from a variety of payment options. Game streaming, on the other hand, is rapidly evolving. While Google Stadia has had a shaky start in the market, Microsoft has announced Xbox Cloud Gaming, available on mobile devices. This brings us one step closer to the metaverse's promise of smooth mobile streaming experiences. Nevertheless, this necessitates a large amount of high-speed data outside of the home, which would necessitate the widespread deployment of high-speed fifth-generation networks (and beyond), which is still a way off.

Open Standards

If the actual Metaverse is to succeed on the internet, it will need to be developed on open standards that link these virtual worlds. This implies that the Metaverse is not "owned" by a single entity, which could be troublesome. This open standard is in direct opposition to Apple and Google's present business models, including walled gardens in which they maintain strict control over payments and what can be published. The dispute between Epic and Apple over Fortnite, which ended in the game being removed from the App Store, is the best example of this. Sweeney's larger objectives for the Metaverse and Epic's role make his willingness to challenge Apple's dominance a possible barrier to a real Metaverse. Finally, the app stores are so profitable for Apple and Google that it would be surprising if they did not adjust to changing market models if their dominance changed.

Recently, mobile games, particularly Chinese applications with specific hangout social spaces, have seen a surge in social functionalities. Mechanics and co-op gameplay are making their way into even simple games. There has been a rising trend in co-op-style tasks over the past three or more years in the top 100 selling iOS mobile apps.

A Functioning Economy

This relates to the preceding argument about the walled garden, notably Apple and Google's desire to control the environment and payment mechanism. Roblox rewards developers with Robux and allows individuals to exchange products, yet it maintains a walled garden. A decentralized economy would be required for a genuine Metaverse to develop. However, we must tread carefully here, given the gaming industry's reaction to blockchain's environmental consequences and NFTs' huge over-inflation and subsequent collapse. Considering the absence of green credentials and the instability of NFTs, blockchain and decentralized finance offer a blueprint for technology initiatives that could help the metaverse's global economy.

Layers of the Metaverse

The value chain of this market is described from the experience that consumers desire to the supporting technology that makes it feasible. More crucially, the concept for a future Metaverse is based on decentralization and fueled. The investments and judgments made today will determine whether this is the future that emerges: one that gives the most extensive range of experiences, powered by artists who make a living doing it—or one characterized by the next round of gatekeepers and rent-takers.

There are seven layers of the Metaverse: Experience, Discovery, Creator Economy, Spatial Computing, Decentralization, Human Interface, and Infrastructure.

Experience

When physical space is dematerialized, what happens? Previously limited experiences may become plentiful. Games show us the way forward: you may pretend to be anybody or whatever you choose in a game. Games will expand to include more live entertainment events, like music concerts and immersive theater, which have already become popular. Sports and internet communities will consist of social entertainment. Meanwhile, traditional industries like tourism, education, and live entertainment will be reshaped to match the abundance and game-thinking virtual economy.

It creates a world in which customers are not only content consumers but also content creators and amplifiers.

Discovery

Most discovery systems may be divided into two categories: inbound and outbound. To begin with, community-driven content is a much more cost-effective source of discovery than other sorts of promotion. If people are enthusiastic about the material or activities they participate in, they will spread the word. As it becomes easier to swap, barter, and distribute content inside more Metaverse circumstances, the content will become a marketing asset in and of itself.

The Metaverse is digitizing social systems in the same way that physical reality is dematerializing. Whereas early phases of the Internet were marked by social media "stickiness" around a few monolithic providers, a decentralized identity ecosystem might give power back to social groups, allowing people to travel frictionlessly between collective experiences.

Creator Economy

Not only are Metaverse experiences becoming more immersive, social, and real-time, but the number of creators is also increasing at a rapid pace. This layer contains all of the technologies that artists use daily to produce consumer-friendly experiences. Previous creator economies followed a typical pattern, whether in the Metaverse, gaming, internet development, or e-commerce:

- **Pioneer era:** The first people to develop experiences for a new technology don't have any tools, so they must start from the ground up. The first websites were written in HTML; users constructed their shopping carts for e-commerce sites, and programmers wrote directly to the graphics hardware for games.

- **Engineering era:** As a result of early successes in the creative business, the number of people on teams explodes. Build-from-scratch is frequently too slow and expensive to meet demand, and as a result, the process becomes more challenging. Early tooling in a market tends to relieve overworked developers by delivering time-saving SDKs and middleware. OpenGL and DirectX are visual frameworks that allow programmers to create 3D graphics without knowing much low-level code.

- **Creator era:** During the creator era, the number of creators has expanded tremendously and enormously. Content creators access tools, templates, and markets that reorient development from a bottom-up, code-oriented approach to a top-down, artistically focused one.

You can now establish an e-commerce website in minutes without knowing a single line of code. Wix and Squarespace are two excellent website-building and maintenance platforms. 3D graphics experiences can be built without ever touching the lower-level rendering APIs using visual interfaces within their studio settings.

Spatial Computing

Spatial computing is a hybrid real/virtual processing that blurs the lines between the physical and ideal worlds. This might take the form of bringing space into the computer or infusing computation into things. Mostly, it means creating systems that push past the usual screen and keyboard constraints without being bogged down in interface or wimpy emulation.

Spatial computing has grown into a broad category of technology that allows us to explore and modify 3D locations and enrich the physical world with additional data and experiences. This comprises the following essential features:

- Geometry and motion are shown using 3D engines (Unity and Unreal)
- Recognition of voice and gestures.
- Data from devices (Internet of Things) and biometrics from humans (for identification and quantified self-applications in health/fitness) are combined.
- User interfaces for the next generation to accommodate many data streams and analysis

Decentralization

The Domain Name System (DNS), which maps individual IP addresses to names and saves you from having to type in a number every time you want to go anywhere online, is the most basic example of decentralization. Distributed computing and microservices enable a scalable environment for developers to access online capabilities—everything from commerce systems to specialized AI to a variety of game systems—without having to worry about constructing or integrating back-end capabilities.

Blockchain technology liberates financial assets from centralized control and custody, and we're already seeing examples of financial legos being connected to construct unique applications in decentralized finance (DeFi). We now witness a series of innovations around decentralized marketplaces and apps for game assets as NFTs and blockchains suited for the type of microtransactions required by games and Metaverse experiences emerge. Computing power will become more like a grid utility (similar to electricity) than a data center.

Human Interface

The closer proximity of computer equipment to our bodies is changing us into cyborgs. Smartphones have outlived their usefulness as phones. They're highly portable, always connected, and powerful PCs with a phone app preloaded. They'll absorb an increasing number of apps and experiences from the Metaverse as downsizing, the correct sensors, embedded AI technologies,

Infrastructure

Our gadgets' infrastructure layer is in charge of enabling them, connecting them to the network, and delivering content. 5G networks will boost capacity while cutting latency and congestion. With 6G, speeds will increase by an order of magnitude. Mobile devices, smart glasses, and wearables in the next generation will need untethered functionality, high performance, and miniaturization, which will necessitate increasingly powerful and tinier hardware: semiconductors that will soon be reduced to 3nm processes and beyond; microelectromechanical systems (MEMS) that will enable tiny sensors; and compact, long-lasting batteries.

Tools

Authoring tools, including apps, behaviors, asset creation, and environment development, must be included in the Metaverse ecosystem. We will see big platforms such as Unity, Unreal, and Autodesk to maintain their dominance and get creative with projects such as EditorXR or MARS. We can also expect more niche offerings like Torch, Sketchbox, and Dotty AR for sharing models, Cognitive3D for analytics, Anything World for voice interaction, and Blippar's Blippbuilder to arise. RealityKit (Apple), Maquette (Microsoft), Spark AR Studio (Meta), Spatial Workstation for immersive audio (Meta via the acquisition of Two Big Ears), Lens Studio (Snap), and Tiltbrush (Google) are just some of the tools that the big tech companies will use to attract creators. Filming and asset development will be enabled by tools such as Digital Catapult's volumetric capture studio Dimension.

What is the best way for individuals to find your product, content, or application after you have generated it? Like today's app stores or search engines, search tools will have to arise, but we may still be too early for that.

Lastly, what types of Metaverse transactions can be expected? The Metaverse will allow the sale of apps or content layers, asset or avatar marketplaces, user trade, ownership of physical-world settings, and, definitely, advertising. Arcona, Database, and AR Grid are just a few of the companies looking into this area.

CHAPTER 3: THE BLOCKCHAIN AND THE METAVERSE

A blockchain is essentially a copied and distributed digital record of transactions across a peer-to-peer network. This means that once a "transaction" is complete, it is forever recorded and irrefutable for all network participants. The number of trusted blocks increases as the network grows, adding to the security. The ledger, which is a digital record of transactions, is decentralized. The group's capability of verification is ingrained. A transaction does not require the approval of a central authority.

Part of the appeal of Bitcoin is that it allows you to send a limitless amount of money across borders without having to worry about Western Union ripping you off on the way out. This is especially important for people of underdeveloped countries and immigrant families who rely on cross-continental money transfers.

Blockchains are categorically open (they are built with open-source software and run in full view of the public); trustless (the network allows participants to interact publicly or privately without the involvement of a trusted third party); and permissionless (Medical records, real estate deeds, tax integrity, statements of work, and even elections will all be tracked via blockchain technology in the future). There are a plethora of possible applications. Blockchains represent digital sovereignty for Web3. They possess the power to control and activate your online persona. Outside of the confines of a platform, a chance to connect, develop, and do business with others. Also, the opportunity to grow as a person.

How the Blockchain Works

The blockchain has a functional scheme based on a distributed register, a database that is made available to all validator nodes present in the network, thus allowing it to decentralize control to the classic server/client models, in which validation takes place at the sole discretion of a central node, hierarchically more authoritative than all the others.

The Components of a Blockchain

A public blockchain is made up of at least five fundamental elements:

- **Nodes:** These are the machines on which the application that allows you to check the status of the registers, blocks, and transactions contained in them is installed. The network of nodes is peer-to-peer in nature, therefore anyone can contribute to its implementation, enjoying the same rights as everyone else, while the management is entrusted to an open-source application that manages every aspect of the functioning of the blockchain.

- **Transaction:** Consists of data relating to a currency exchange, the stipulation/deposit of a contract, and other agreements, regardless of their legal value. The details of the transaction are validated with cryptographic tools and stored in the blocks.

- **Block:** They contain the validated transactions and are concatenated by a cryptographic value that binds a single block to the next, forming a chain of blocks (blockchain).

- **Ledger:** Public ledger containing validated blocks.
- **Hash:** An operation based on asymmetric cryptography, which allows you to irreversibly encode a string of text/numbers, so that any node can verify its validity, without being able to explicitly read the content of the transaction. The hash is used at various moments in the constitution of the chain and returns a code that makes each element unique. Among the main cryptographic algorithms used we find the SHA-256

At the operational level, various moments intervene from the onset of a transaction to the archiving of a block, subject to validation based on non-discretionary cryptographic elements. This allows for a condition of impartiality that does not force the nodes to have to trust each other's work. If there are anomalies, the very nature of the elements will immediately reveal them, invalidating the suspicious blocks. So let's see how the single transaction is formed and how it becomes part of a block in the chain.

The most common form of transaction on a blockchain is characterized by a transfer of digital currency, such as Bitcoin, between two parties. The transaction is backed up by double key encryption. A private key, which allows the two parties to access and make available the quantity of Bitcoin agreed for the exchange, and a public key, which encrypts the transaction to allow validation.

The great freedom offered by the blockchain, therefore, has a price, as the related services deal with managing the flow of transactions, but they can do nothing in controlling the possession of resources.

Once closed, a transaction must be placed in a block to be archived. The proposer submits their transaction to the reference blockchain, paying a commission for the computational work that the validators must perform during the proof of work. In Bitcoin, a new block is issued every ten minutes, which on average contains 2,000 to 3,000 transactions. In peak periods, there may be many transactions to be archived and, in this case, the system will proceed giving priority to those with the highest commission, leaving the others waiting.

The security of the blockchain is guaranteed practically at all levels, from the democratic system that rules it to the open-source code of the management application that makes the rules of the game clear, up to the massive presence of cryptography at every stage, which makes manipulation absolutely unlikely. Private individuals must pay close attention to the retention of their access data.

DLT and blockchain are also enabling technologies of the Internet of Value (IoV) a concept proposed by Ripple, which envisages transferring value with operational methods and simplicity typical of data transfer in the Internet of Things (IoT).

Distributed Ledger Technologies (DLT)

DLT are decentralized systems based on a distributed ledger. All nodes in the network have the same version of the registry. They can read and modify it, but for a new version to be universally adopted, it must be subjected to a distributed consensus, which is obtained when at least 50% of the nodes in the network express a favorable opinion.

DLTs allow registry changes governed by open-source consensus algorithms, which can be verified by anyone. Validations usually take place by solving mathematical problems, working tests useful for verifying and validating the contents of transactions through cryptographic techniques that require considerable computational calculation.

Blockchain systems are also distinguished by being characterized by assets such as cryptocurrencies and for the management of transactions of a simple nature, such as the transfer of money, or complex, such as the regulation of contracts (smart contracts).

Tokens and ICO, What They Are, and What Relationship They Have With the Blockchain

Younger audiences likely associate phone booths with the place where Clark Kent steps out of, as Superman, rather than a prized red street ornament on the London scene. The older of us will rather remember the times when telephone tokens were used inside those booths. There was no mobile telephony, let alone the blockchain, yet tokens were already a reality widely used to create an element of value to be used to purchase service.

Each token gave the right to a conversation period, deducted according to the rates in force. Like meal vouchers, another example of an "analog" token, they are equivalent to a certain amount of money to be spent in the affiliated centers. How did we go from the classic token to cryptocurrency?

What Are Unpermissioned (or Permissionless) Blockchains

Otherwise known as public, permissionless blockchains are based on registers that anyone is allowed to access, to the point that every node in the network keeps an integral copy of them. They are decentralized by nature and governed by the distributed consent rule, to prevent anyone from becoming the exclusive owner and exercising direct control, such as censoring a transaction.

Public blockchains are particularly suitable where there is a fundamental need for immutability and security, as in the case of cryptocurrencies, ownership contracts.

Otherwise known as private, permissioned blockchains are governed by an invitation, strictly conditioned by the acceptance of certain rules.

Private Blockchains, therefore, constitute an effective model to meet the specific needs of companies and in general for any context in which the public nature is not compatible with data management policies. The private nature allows you to bypass a series of processes that are in fact indispensable to guarantee the impartiality of the operations of a public blockchain and this basically allows much greater efficiency, in the face of a decidedly reduced computational requirement.

A private blockchain can be programmed in a single company, or be based on a consortium, widespread infrastructures, especially in the field of finance, to group a series of members who share databases relating to some services or products. It is an intermediate condition between the total control of a private blockchain and the possibility of exploiting the advantages of the public network.

Among the best-known Blockchain Consortia, we find HyperLedger, supported by IBM and Linux Foundation; EEA (Enterprise Ethereum Alliance), backed by Ethereum and, among others, Microsoft and JPMorgan. A particular case is constituted by Ripple, which although not a consortium but a public blockchain, capable of self-financing thanks to the homonymous cryptocurrency (XRP), actually manages a series of banking consortia that use its business software.

Bitcoin is what is called a public blockchain, which anyone can access, unconditionally accepting the rules.

What Are Blockchain Tokens and How They Work

Fungible Tokens

This is the case of cryptocurrencies, but more generally of any currency, digital or not, which by nature, can be exchanged for something identical. In the case of a banknote, this is characterized by a value, but to make a payment it is not necessary to use a specific banknote. Any banknote with that value will do. Compared to traditional currencies, regulated by central banks, cryptocurrencies are regulated by their respective blockchains. Blockchain technology also allows you to create other fungible tokens, such as stablecoins, CBDCs (Central Bank Digital Currency), reputation tokens, and, in general, programmable coins.

Non-Fungible Tokens

This is the case of unique objects and entities, which cannot be exchanged for something identical. In the traditional context, we could identify a real estate property, land, a work of art.

Applications and Examples of the Use of the Blockchain

After so much theory, so many definitions and so many concepts, here we are, finally, at a review of blockchain applications, to understand how and where this emerging technology is today the protagonist and where we will see it conquer an increasingly relevant space in the years that await us.

The following list constitutes only a part of the possible applications and has been selected to highlight even those areas in which the use of a blockchain could radically change the current scenario, even in the absence of currently relevant case studies.

The Blockchain in Banks and Financial Products

Financial services are arguably the most advanced sector.

In the case of payments, for example, peer-to-peer technology can be used to transfer funds between different banks, enabling new options as regards the clearing and settlement methods for assets, securities, and derivatives. The blockchain allows for automated and much safer transactions, radically simplifying the management and the consequent risk of spreading counterfeit securities. The issuance of security on the blockchain allows you to manage the entire life cycle of the security in a much more agile way in the various operations envisaged: distribution of dividends, voting rights, etc.

The Blockchain in the Insurance Market

Blockchain technology enables a wide range of options, for example for the decentralized management of a policy, capable of significantly reducing both the complexity and the activation and management costs, also eliminating the need for intermediation. Many operations can be automated: the calculation of prices, the system of expertise and claims, obtaining and ensuring the insured maximum transparency at every stage.

The Blockchain in the Agrifood Sector

The food supply chain is in all probability the most complex of all, as the number of players and products involved is extremely high, as is the number of relationships that are structured through the life stages of the product, from its cultivation/breeding up to consumption on the table. But the blockchain is starting to ease and make the register of all these relationships much more efficient, especially in terms of security and transparency for all stakeholders.

The Blockchain for Industry 4.0

In the generic context of Industry 4.0, the blockchain is part of the applications of various enabling technologies, obviously starting from IT security. Its use is decidedly transversal and goes from the management of the supply chain, regulating contracts with suppliers and tracking the goods, simultaneously enabling new strategies for quality control.

The Blockchain in Healthcare

The natural inclination to optimize services makes the blockchain a very interesting tool for healthcare. For example, direct payment for services, which can be automated and customized for each user registered in the system, also streamlining the necessary authentication procedures to dedicated platforms. Another very interesting area lies in the certification of ownership of medical records, with a unique identifier, managed as an immutable transaction.

Doctors can directly certify the communications between the various IoT devices with which they are called to interact, making any diagnostic procedure absolutely transparent, which cannot be changed in its history. For example, this reduces the risk of manipulating medical records if they were recorded through a DLT. Tracking properties apply to the complex and costly supply chain of medicines and hospital supplies, where too often we see inappropriate speculation.

The Blockchain in the Pharmaceutical Industry

In the case of the drug, the blockchain contributes decisively to the supply chain, above all to avoid the phenomenon of counterfeiting and fraud.

The Blockchain in Public Administration

In addition to reducing the number of human resources necessary for the provision of many services, the blockchain would also allow an enormous motivational factor for public employees, who would see the results of their work transparently tracked, also in relation to the achievement of performance objectives annually, which in their traditional conception are difficult to monitor and evaluate.

The Blockchain in Logistics

With the blockchain it is possible to uniquely track goods during transport and storage in the warehouse, drastically reducing the possibility of errors on the inventories.

The Blockchain in the GDO

The entire supply chain could be managed more safely and efficiently.

The Blockchain in Energy

Smart contracts are contributing significantly to the innovation of energy distribution, enabling new exchange processes, starting with those between the distributors themselves, which can take place in peer-to-peer mode. Smart contracts also enable electric vehicle charging systems, thanks to micropayment solutions, as well as eliminating the intermediation processes traditionally required to activate and manage energy supply contracts.

The Blockchain in the Electoral System

The management of the voting procedure through a smart contract makes a system otherwise very complex to regulate and monitor much easier, especially to avoid the phenomenon of double voting, which the blockchain could manage in a similar way to what happens in financial transactions for the double-spending phenomenon.

The Blockchain in Intellectual Property

The distributed register of the blockchain is an ideal tool for filing patents, also by virtue of the dynamics linked to their conservation.

The Blockchain in Retail

Retail is currently undergoing a radical transformation of the sales and services model, in the orbit of an omnichannel strategy towards which all product brands are aligning. The blockchain, beyond making the supply chain of goods safer and more efficient, is increasing customer loyalty through customized programs, which aim to reward and encourage consumption.

The Blockchain in Gaming

Blockchain technologies make it possible to enable strategies in the field of gaming, thanks to the possibility of acquiring payments and rewarding registered players in cryptocurrency or through PayPal, due to the time spent or the scores achieved.

Games are in fact a relevant example of distributed applications (dApps), starting from the second generation of blockchain. Popular blockchain games include Splinterlands (on HIVE blockchain), Crypto Dynasty (EOS), Upland (EOS), Prospector (WAX), IOI-game (Tron), and Chain Clash (ETH).

The Blockchain in the Art

NFTs are literally revolutionizing the art market. The possibility of making a unique digital work has contributed to giving value to goods that otherwise, due to their natural reproducibility, would be completely lacking value.

This phenomenon has meant that many artists have begun to tokenize their digital works on special platforms (SuperRare, Rarible, Foundation, etc.) that regulate the market, recognizing the creator for royalty for each subsequent transaction.

The Blockchain in **Charitable Initiatives**

The blockchain makes it possible to track the money donated and verify that subsequent transactions lead them to an effective destination. In an even more transparent way, the charity could envisage a smart contract capable of self-regulating, effectively disbursing the donated sum only upon the occurrence of certain conditions, known a priori, to offer total guarantee and transparency to the benefactor.

The Blockchain in the Arms Market

The possibility of uniquely identifying an asset could contribute to a large extent to limiting the illegal arms trade, allowing counterfeits introduced on the market to be checked in a much simpler and more immediate way.

Metaverse and Blockchain, a Possible Combination

Although not begun at the same time, Metaverse and blockchain could represent a valid combination for the development of 3D virtual worlds. Environments that we could define as "Metaverses developed on blockchain architecture" are demonstrating some interesting potential that makes them decidedly attractive (also in economic terms with the interest of many investors) compared to the 3D virtual worlds known to date in the gaming world.

The so-called Metaverse blockchains could give rise to new business models by influencing, for example, real estate markets (effectively expanding the concept of "virtual real estate"), the creation of digital assets (including NFTs), and new ways of enjoying digital/virtual events.

CHAPTER 4: THE BLOCKCHAIN AND THE DEFI

What Is Decentralized Finance?

Decentralized finance or DeFi as it is abbreviated, is a term used for several applications and projects that are developed on a blockchain impacting traditional finance. DeFi are peer-to-peer applications developed on blockchain networks and decentralized refers to not requiring access rights to facilitate loans, oracles, cryptocurrencies, swaps, derivatives, and other financial tools.

The emergence of this type of finance is due to our history, before, we exchanged goods and services, but the economy has evolved, different levels of it were created. Some currencies have had more confidence than others, but all have been centralized which makes them more vulnerable to devaluations. But with DeFi is developed as a base to have an open financial system with the purpose of not having a central authority.

DeFi is an entire ecosystem of applications and working protocols that delivers value to millions of users. More than $30 billion is locked up in DeFi ecosystems. Therefore, they are a high-growth segment.

In terms of the future of this type of technology, we have seen a quantum leap in the way people invest. It is difficult to predict how this space will be configured when the power to create financial services is democratized. But looking empirically, every day there is more trust and more people are betting on making a profit.

The DeFi mentality is pretty simple. Banks and other financial institutions provide a whole host of services, from wealth storage, loans, facilitating transactions, etc. DeFi aims to replace these services one by one with a crypto alternative (each service having its cryptocurrency).

Many could argue that Bitcoin will replace the currency, security, and store of value (among other things), but what about other products banks offer like interest-yielding savings accounts, pension investments, or loans? DeFi can replace each of these services one by one. The DeFi "movement," if you will, sets out to find more decentralized, efficient, and fair financial products.

For this reason, people are looking for alternatives, not because people have something against banks (although many in the crypto world do), it's because they can feel the price of assets running away from them. They are looking to the crypto world with its massive growth as a place for at least securing, if not growing, their wealth at a pace to keep up with the destruction of purchasing power of traditional currencies.

Especially now, the government printing presses have gone into overdrive mode, some even predicting a colossal crash of traditional currencies (or just eternal inflation). Even if you're not in that doomsday camp, it's fair to say, at the very least, the value of assets priced in dollars and other government-backed currencies has been growing and will continue to grow faster than your pay-chcck.

DeFi aims to create financial products that don't rely on gambling in the crypto exchanges with one coin or another. It treats cryptocurrency as real money and is as serious in the business of money as the traditional banking sector is. People are already earning reasonable interest rates safely in many other ways mentioned before using stable coins. Cryptocurrencies and DeFi are taking away the services that the financial sector used to have a monopoly. One such service is certificates of deposit (sometimes known as time deposits), and it is this service that Hex is the first crypto alternative.

Advantages of DeFi

Transparency

Just to be clear, transparency doesn't mean that everyone else on the blockchain can see what you personally have done or invested in. Users are identified by a string of alphanumeric characters that can't be traced to you in real life.

Independence from Traditional Financial Structures

Many modern money applications are strictly regulated, especially in the US and Europe. At first, plenty of early adopters latched onto crypto as a way to escape financial scrutiny and to make purchases on the "dark web." Sites on the dark web (or "deep web") are typically encrypted in a way that they don't appear on traditional search engines.

Global Solutions

There's no real reason other than current infrastructure that people should only access capital from the country that they live in, or buy things from the country (or region) that they live in. Wealthy people can easily buy whatever they want across the world, and hire someone to do all the tedious work to make that possible. The rest of us don't live in that reality.

Customizable User Experience

Technology does tend to expect that the early adopters have some knowledge. As applications and systems become more mainstream and more non-techies need to use them, the apps become much friendlier to all users.

Blockchain

It is part of a huge revolution, not only in the economy but in all areas. I'm going to explain it in a simple way for you to understand its function. Let's start by knowing what a blockchain is. Imagine that Pedro wants to send Carlos a thousand euros, normally he does it through a bank transfer. The bank is the intermediary between the parties. In a period of time, depending on the bank, the money arrives at Carlos's account and subtracts one thousand to Pedro.

Here everything is easy and hassle-free, but... there is a but. Neither Pedro nor Carlos have control over the process, only the banks have all the information, they are subject to their conditions and commissions where applicable, of course.

That's where blockchain comes in, eliminates the intermediaries, and decentralizes the whole process. The process is now up to Pedro and Carlos. The blockchain is a huge ledger where the records or blocks are linked and encrypted to protect the security and privacy of transactions. Here there must be several users or nodes that are responsible for verifying the transactions to validate them and that the block corresponding to the transaction is recorded in the ledger.

Now, Pedro and Carlos are not alone, they are part of a huge group of users who are responsible for checking the process. If Pedro withdraws a Bitcoin from the account to give it to Carlos, he first notifies everyone of this process, no one knows who Pedro or Carlos is, they only know that from a wallet that sum is transferred to another.

Then when Peter is going to send the sum, he notifies others, checks that there is that asset to send, the transaction is noted and completed and becomes part of that block of transactions. As time goes by, more and more transactions are completed in the block, which has limited capacity, depending on the chain structure and size of the transaction. When a block can't support any more transactions, it's time to seal it or validate it, which is what bitcoin miners do.

Mining is a series of complex calculations that require time and electricity, but when it is permanently recorded on the blockchain, it is an operation that also requires the majority of nodes to validate it.

So, blockchain is a mathematical structure that stores data in a way that is almost impossible to falsify. Each record is called a block and allows an open, user-controlled group of users to participate in that electronic ledger.

Blockchain is only updated under the consensus of the system participants when they enter new data. It can never be deleted.

Let's take a look at one of its advantages:

- **Security:** One of its biggest benefits is that it is an ultra-secure network because the data is transmitted encrypted, which is more secure than the standard password and username system. Decentralized data using blockchain makes it very difficult to hack because all documents are stored on thousands of different hard drives, reducing the likelihood of data loss.

Smart Contracts and Decentralization

- You can pay bills, get paid on time, reduce the need for middlemen and outside organizations, information is distributed throughout the network. Governments can no longer shut down the sources they want to repress because the information exists on many computers through the network.
- Efficient and fast manually entering data is tedious and time-consum-

ing. Organizations have many systems of record for various tasks. With blockchain, everything is stored and verified as it is generated. The speed of verification has great benefits, a simple stock purchase can take up to a week to verify using current methods.

- Blockchain has no need for third-party verification, everything is there, verifiable and in plain sight. It represents a new paradigm for the way information is shared and companies are rushing to figure out how to use distributed accounting technology to save time and administration costs.

Token

It is a unit of value that goes beyond central banks. The most famous token is Bitcoin, which is based on blockchain technology; it is followed by more and more tokens with high probabilities.

Is there a difference between a token, a cryptocurrency, a digital currency, and virtual currencies? Yes, although they are often used synonymously to refer to cryptocurrencies, let's clarify each one.

About cryptocurrencies, Bitcoin or ether are two examples of what they are. Bitcoin operates on its original blockchain of creation. Ether is used within its own blockchain. They can be sent, received, and mined.

They tend to have the same characteristics as money, they can be fungible, divided, and their creation has certain limits (different in Ether and Bitcoin). Its purpose is to be able to pay for goods and services. But not only have that but also as a store of valued (Bitcoin) and generation of services through dApps and DeFi.

The concept of cryptocurrency includes the altcoins, which are so-called because they would come to occupy the place of alternative to Bitcoin. Many altcoins are forks of Bitcoin and were developed using its open-source code. Examples of these are Litecoin, Dogecoin, and others.

Now, tokens are digital assets that can be used within the ecosystem of a given project. They differ from cryptocurrencies because the former requires the blockchain to function. Ethereum is the most common platform for creating tokens, mainly because of its smart contracts. The tokens that are created on the Ethereum blockchain are known as ERC-20 tokens, e.g. Tether.

The purpose of tokens is different from cryptocurrencies, although they can be used to pay.

A digital currency is a general term used to describe all forms of electronic money, be it virtual currency, or cryptocurrencies, although they are not the same. The defining characteristic of digital currencies is that they only exist electronically, unlike banknotes or coins.

Cryptocurrency is also a differentiator for cryptocurrencies, meaning it is encrypted to make scams like counterfeiting more difficult.

Now, virtual currencies, although digital by definition, are different. The European Central Bank defines it as digital money in an unregulated environment, issued and controlled by its developers, used as a method of payment between members of a specific community.

It's a great example, they are not based specifically on cryptocurrencies, but on others, like video games, such as World of Warcraft tokens, GTA V Online cash cards, or FIFA points from EA Sports games.

Smart contracts make it possible to automate contractual relationships between people or machines without the intervention of trusted intermediaries.

Distributed databases where blockchain ensures that all information is visible, without waiting to see if the other party is honest. The data cannot be falsified, making it ideal for smart contracts.

Computers play an important role in smart contracts. Not only do they store data or enable electronic signatures, but they also perform analysis and implement some of the parts of their internal logic.

How to Enter DeFi?

In order to get into DeFi investments, first, we need to know some tools where to buy cryptocurrencies. These are the three main ones, let's know their advantages and disadvantages.

Binance

Binance launched its ICO on July 3 and put up for sale 100 million ERC20 tokens called BNB (Binance Coin). It lasted just 3 minutes and managed to raise $15 million. 11 days after launching the ICO the exchange was already available.

There were many registered users after the launch, which generated some access problems due to the large volume of users. Today it is valued at more than two billion dollars.

If we look at the Binance menu we find a series of options for each of its tasks:

- **Exchange:** To exchange cryptocurrencies, where real-time analysis of the market will appear.
- **Academy:** Cryptocurrency education. Courses, tutorials, and more on the subject.
- **BCF:** This is a blockchain charitable foundation. Information about the company's charities and donations.
- **Info:** It has information about cryptocurrencies, such as exchange rates, traded volumes, and costs.
- **Labs:** It is an incubator for outstanding blockchain projects. This is where the company's team that will develop blockchain solutions is located.
- **Launch pad:** This is a platform for users to launch their own tokens.
- **Research:** Has information about the company, about the mission, tasks, and who they are.
- **Trust wallet:** This is an official cryptocurrency wallet.

It also has another series of folding menus on the upper right side. There a number of options appear:

- **Funds:** Deposits, withdrawals, balances, withdrawal and deposit histories, and credit card purchases.
- **Order management:** You have open orders, order history, and transaction history.
- **Careers:** Application for studies with the academy.
- **Support:** Information on common problems with users and solutions.
- **News:** Recent publications in the press about the company and other related topics.

Bit2Me

The entire system is developed internally by its operators and considers both a technological and commercial enterprise, creating products, processes, and tools to change the world, with the goal of enabling frictionless, fair, and transparent markets.

Among its functions we can find:

- Cryptocurrency wallet.
- It has a trading platform.
- Bit2me Pay.
- Crypto payments can be accepted in the business.
- It has secure cryptocurrency custody.
- Tikebit.
- MasterCard to pay some cryptocurrencies.
- Exclusive services for clients.

You have to create an account, before trading, you have to go through a data validation process. It is a process that you achieve quickly. To be able to use it you need to have set up the profile well, filled in all the data, and attached your ID. It is an important step in this kind of platform.

Some do not trust this step, but the truth is that these operations are banking and you must have your information here. If you become a millionaire, you can put on a face and then pay taxes like a good citizen. Another feature is that you have recently incorporated in Bit2Me Trade, for people who are new to the world of trading or for professionals.

It's not just for buying cryptocurrencies though. It is a team of people who provide knowledge and value to the community. This world is very wide and needs people to clarify all the information. They have their project called Academy, where they provide a lot of valuable information. It is a reliable exchange, although as confident as they are you should not trust your assets to any exchange, the good thing is that they share the same opinion. If you invest a lot to save and leave it in an external wallet, you should not have the money in the blockchain.

Coinbase

It is a great platform that offers you many advantages. Among them, you can see the graphs with the evolution of prices, you can know how the value of the cryptocurrencies you have goes up or down. Let's analyze this platform in detail.

To register is very easy, you just need to be of legal age, give the service the name, surname, email, and password, and you can make use of the account. Then you link another payment method that can be a PayPal account, bank, credit, or debit card.

Coinbase can be used on mobile or the website. You can see the fiat money value of your investments, the evolution of the main cryptos, and decide which ones you want to be shown to you, seeing a summary of the outstanding news of the sector. There is a button called Trade, where you can buy, sell or convert cryptocurrencies. In any of the cases before accepting the operation will always appear the commission you have to pay so that everything is clear to you.

You will also see a bar with options like Portfolio, where you can know the status of the assets, seeing the money you have in the various cryptos and the evolution. In Coinbase the information also appears on the home page and is deliberately in Portfolio.

You also find the Pricing section, where you can see the current status of the assets that Coinbase allows you to manage, both what you have bought and what you haven't bought. It will tell you the current state of the market in general, the value of the assets in real-time, how much you have gone up or down with respect to the value of each asset in the last 24 hours.

You also have the settings section where you can add payment methods or make invitations to earn euro balance by getting others to sign up. You can set your local currency or purchase limits, which can be set to an amount of money per day in the steps or to spend without control what you want. You can set a PIN to protect the application, notifications, privacy, or email.

CHAPTER 5: CRYPTOCURRENCY EXPLAINED IN 5 MINUTES

What Is Cryptocurrency?

Cryptocurrency is a digital currency that is encrypted to prevent counterfeiting and double-spending. Several cryptocurrencies use blockchain technology, a distributed ledger enforced by a distributed network of computers. Cryptocurrencies differ from traditional currencies in that they are not issued by central authorities, potentially making them immune to government intervention or manipulation.

Cryptocurrencies are online payment systems using virtual "tokens" to represent ledger entries on the system's internal ledger. The phrase "crypto" refers to various encryption methods and cryptographic approaches, such as elliptical curve encryption, public-private key pairs, and hashing algorithms.

In plain English, Cryptocurrencies are online payment systems that use virtual "tokens" to enable safe transactions. Cryptocurrency can be purchased using crypto exchanges such as Coinbase, Cash App, **etc.**

Cryptocurrencies have the potential of making it easier to send money between two people without requiring a trusted third party like banks or credit card providers. Instead, these transfers are secured by public and private keys and different incentive systems like Proof of Work and Proof of Stake.

A user's "wallet," or address, in modern cryptocurrency networks, has a public key, while the private key is known solely by the owner and used to sign transactions. Users can avoid the substantial fees banks and other financial institutions charge for wire transfers by completing fund transactions with minimal processing charges.

Crypto in the Metaverse

Cryptocurrencies skyrocketed after Facebook CEO Mark Zuckerberg announced the company's rebranding as Meta. Digital currencies will play an important role in the Metaverse because they share a fundamental operational principle: decentralization of fiscal ownership, which allows for verifiable and immutable ownership of virtual assets.

To attend the digital concert, your digital avatar may require some fancy attire. So, what kind of monetary exchanges will take place in the virtual world? Cryptocurrency is the answer to a virtual economy's demand for money.

The Metaverse will be dominated by blockchains and cryptocurrencies. Transactions will be cryptographically secured on a blockchain.

NFTs, which are essentially unique digital goods—pieces of art or in-game items, for example—where the ownership and other information are recorded into the token, have sparked interest in digital properties. Currently, gamers can establish their own virtual casinos and use cryptocurrencies to monetize them.

NFTs will allow users control of their characters, in-game purchases, and even the ability to register virtual territories in their names in the Metaverse. In the virtual economy, cryptocurrencies will become legal cash, and all intangible objects will be NFTs.

Crypto is a requirement because of the ease of use it provides, which is fueled by developing technology and the demand for transparency. People will be more confident in making more and better investments and trade as a result of this. This will be accomplished by combining cryptography with virtual reality and augmented reality technology. With the help of NFTs, it might become the only tender for use in the Metaverse.

In order to ensure that the transactional history is valid, most cryptocurrencies use blockchains, which are organizational systems that ensure that the transactional history is real. As a result, blockchains are critical components of the majority of digital currencies. Following the adoption of blockchain technology, according to banking and finance industry experts, various challenges will arise across several areas, including financial services and the legal profession, in the not-to-distant future. In contrast, cryptocurrencies like Bitcoin and Ethereum have come under fire for a number of reasons, including their usage in criminal activities and their high volatility. Despite this, they have received high appreciation for a number of reasons, including their mobility, capacity to be separated, inflation resistance, and clarity, among others.

Bitcoin is also a kind of money that allows you to conduct secure online payments, which is another benefit. Cryptocurrencies are represented by virtual 'tokens,' which means they don't really exist and are represented by ledger entries that are created internally inside the network to represent them in order for them to be represented. When it comes to overseeing such ledger entries, cryptography is a phrase that refers to the many encryption methods and cryptographic procedures that are used. Examples of cryptography include, among other things, elliptical curve encryption, public-private key pairs, and hashing techniques. The fact that cryptocurrencies such as Bitcoin are not true money has not deterred many people from hailing them as the beginning of a new financial epoch.

And are you aware of the fact that, in order to get extra dollars or transfer monies to others in the future, you will need access to an ATM or a bank connection? If you conduct all of your transactions entirely via the use of cryptocurrencies, you may be able to totally remove the necessity for banks and other centralized intermediaries in your transactional interactions. Given the fact that cryptocurrencies are built on a technology known as the blockchain, which serves as a decentralized database, as previously said, this is the situation (meaning no single entity is in charge of it). Instead, every computer linked to the network confirms that the transactions that have taken place have in fact taken place by running a series of tests. First and foremost, while trading your chicken for a pair of shoes in the past days, recall that the products you were dealing with had intrinsic worth that was inherent in their very nature, as opposed to today's situation.

But when money in the form of coins, bills of exchange (cash), and credit cards became more widespread in everyday life, the notion of money, and perhaps more importantly, the trust model connected with money, underwent a substantial transformation. As far as the simplicity with which money may now be moved from one person to another is concerned, substantial advancements have been achieved in recent years. The difficulties of transferring a metric tonne of gold bars from one country to another across international borders was a motivating factor behind the development of money, in part because of the logistical challenges involved. In the aftermath, individuals became even more sedentary than they had been before, which enabled the development of credit cards to become a reality. Payments made with a credit card are subject to the laws and regulations of your country; payments made with a debit card are not subject to the laws and regulations of your government.

Learn About Bitcoin

Bitcoin is a cryptocurrency that exists in the realm of digital or virtual money, and it is denominated in Bitcoins. Bitcoin is digital money, sometimes known as a virtual currency. It is digital or virtual money that is safeguarded by encryption, making it almost impossible to forge or double spend with the cash in circulation. Many cryptocurrencies rely on the operation of a decentralized network based on blockchain technology in order to function correctly. Blockchain technology is a distributed ledger that is maintained by a distributed network of computers that is located in different locations. Additionally, blockchain technology is being used by a huge variety of cryptocurrencies in order to simplify the operation of their respective systems.

Given the fact that cryptocurrencies are not issued by a centralized body, it is theoretically plausible that they will be impervious to intervention or manipulation by government authorities in the future. Another one of cryptocurrency's most distinctive traits is that it does not have a central bank to rely on for liquidity. Comparatively speaking to the other forms of digital assets now available, a cryptocurrency is a digital asset produced by a network of computers and distributed among a large number of nodes, and it is referred to as such. Decentralized organizations are able to operate independently of governments and other centralized entities due to the fact that they are decentralized. The word "cryptocurrency" refers to the encryption technologies used to protect networks from unauthorized access and use. This term is derived from the encryption technologies used to protect networks from unauthorized access and usage.

It is less complicated to transact with cryptocurrencies across several accounts than it is to trade with fiat money across many accounts. In order to complete the transaction, it is possible to utilize internet-connected devices such as PCs, tablet computers, and cellphones, among other things. In order to avoid problems, it will be necessary to deal with fiat money in person or via the same financial institution as cryptocurrency. As an added bonus, since they will be stored on the Internet, you will not be needed to bring them with you when you go to your destination in person. This gives you the freedom to go anywhere with a stable Internet connection and to take your cryptocurrencies with you, independent of the current market value of those coins in your possession. Extreme value storage should only be used on products that have the potential to maintain essentially constant levels of usefulness or pleasure over an extended period of time, such as musical instruments.

The Effect of Metaverse on Cryptos

Asymmetric hedges against real-world occurrences are virtual earnings. The Virtual Economy thrives when things are going well. When things go wrong, though, it may succeed as a location for education, entertainment, community, utility, and sports, unaffected by social distance or depleting hand sanitizer supplies. We will see new symbols, influencers, and businesses emerge from this global confinement within virtual worlds. They will rise to prominence at a time when established institutions, customs, and the social contract are being called into doubt. The Virtual Economy is forming as natural ventilation for a social system that is now unstable and broken.

These platforms are the brains of the virtual economy. They function as centers for entertainment, content creation, social interaction, and, on rare occasions, economic production, and exchange. These platforms are rapidly growing in popularity.

CHAPTER 6: COMPOUND CRYPTO

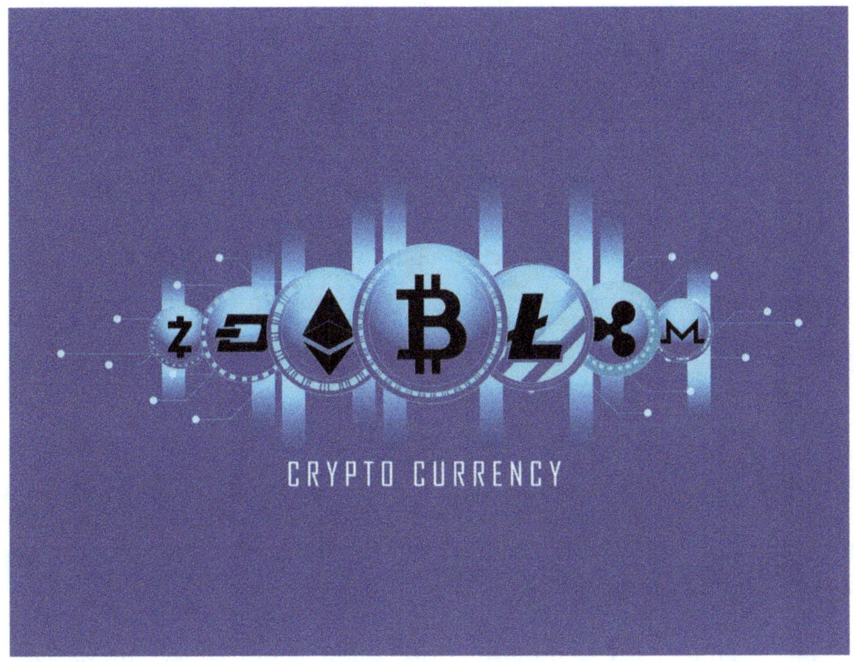

Who are the Metaverse players in the cryptocurrency space?

Starting with the most established players, the largest market caps we've got are Axie, Decentraland, Sandbox, and Enjin, or safe mid-cap cryptos.

Axie Infinity

It is a game where you can buy, train and breed Pokémon-like creatures that are themselves NFTs. Each is individually registered on the Ethereum blockchain. Just like any other NFT, you can trade and sell your Axie on the marketplace for cryptocurrencies.

The SandBox

The blockchain gaming sector has seen explosive growth throughout 2021. As non-fungible tokens and play-to-earn gaming help create new income opportunities for people around the globe while also ushering in a new cohort of users to the crypto space. One project that is deeply involved in gaming and building its advanced Metaverse structure is the SandBox.

For both Decentraland and the Sandbox, you have complete control over your in-world creations. No centralized platforms to restrict what you can or can't do. That's one of the benefits of blockchain.

Netvrk

Netvrk is still a relatively young project, but I find its Metaverse ecosystem fascinating. Netvrk is a Metaverse focus project founded by Michael Katseli, Linus Chee, and Ian Friend.

Netvrk describes itself as "a social virtual world and platform with powerful creation tools and infrastructure to create, share, experience and monetize creation easily."

Netvrk's primary goal is to allow users to leverage NFTs and in-game land tokens to generate passive revenue by leasing their property or selling their NFTs, thus creating an entirely Metaverse-centric economy. Furthermore, this Metaverse project lets users buy assets within its virtual domain, including buildings, offices, vehicles, houses, and pretty much anything you can think of.

Decentraland

This is a virtual world built on Ethereum where users can buy and develop plots of virtual land, create artworks, etc. These assets come in the form of unique NFTs that can be traded on the marketplace. Have you ever played the Sims or Second Life? Well, you're looking at a blockchain version of these classics.

The Decentraland platform with MANA tokens allows its players to purchase portions of land and use them to build/realize what they most desire (concerts, recreational spaces, land used for car driving tests). The owners of these assets are able to get real gains generated by the value imported by all users who interact with them. MANA token holders also have the right to vote on any changes that are proposed for the system, since it is based on DAO (Decentralized Autonomous Organization) technology.

Where you can buy:

https://www.etoro.com

https://www.binance.com/it

Enjin Coin

This crypto is the oil that lubricates the Enjin platform, an all-in-one suite of tools that allow users to create NFTs on the Ethereum blockchain and integrate them into games and apps. Beyond the well-known staples, you can do your research and discover many up-and-coming projects with good use cases.

We'll list a few of them, so first, we've got Effinity (EFI), a blockchain dedicated to NFTs developed by Enjin built on Polkadot. There is more to say about Polkadot, which will be discussed as we proceed.

OVR

You've OVR, a digital layer covering the entire world comprising 1.6 trillion pieces of land. All of them are individual NFTs that you can buy and sell. They're essentially creating the first google earth on the blockchain.

Metaverse Index (MVI)

This token allows investors to invest in the world of cryptocurrencies related to the Metaverse without participating in gaming activities or virtual gaming platforms. In fact, investors can leverage the MVI token as a true ETF for the Crypto Metaverse, capturing tokens that offer various services in virtual reality environments. However, the tokens must be developed on the Ethereum blockchain and their capitalization must be greater than $50 million.

Somnium Space (CUBE)

In Somnium Space it is possible to create, buy and exchange digital worlds and NFT resources. The peculiarity of this system, based on CUBE tokens, is the fact that before making purchases or exchanges, users can experience and try the virtual worlds created. It will be possible to dine in a restaurant designed by another player or visit an exhibition in a museum. CUBE is also based on the Ethereum blockchain and is an ERC-20 utility token.

Metahero

You can use their 3d scanner to create your digital avatar. It is another 3d NFT that can be used across games, VR, social media, and online fashion. So imagine using your 3d avatar to try out clothes that you might be interested in quickly.

Where Can You Buy These Metaverse Cryptocurrencies?

Well, the largest staples can be bought on any centralized exchanges such as Binance and Coinbase. You can also buy them inside DeFi as well. For example, the Ethereum based tokens can all be picked up on an old uni swap but watch out for the gas fees. The Binance smart chain tokens can be bought from a good old pancake swap. Now, if you're ever in doubt, just search up the token on coinmarketcap.com or coingecko.com and then go to the market tab. It will tell you all the centralized and decentralized exchanges trading the token.

I've got some of these cryptocurrencies on exchanges for trading and staking in Binance. Currently, I'm staking some Sandbox, Axie Infinity, and a bunch of other things in the lock staking pools on Binance, and it is effortless to do.

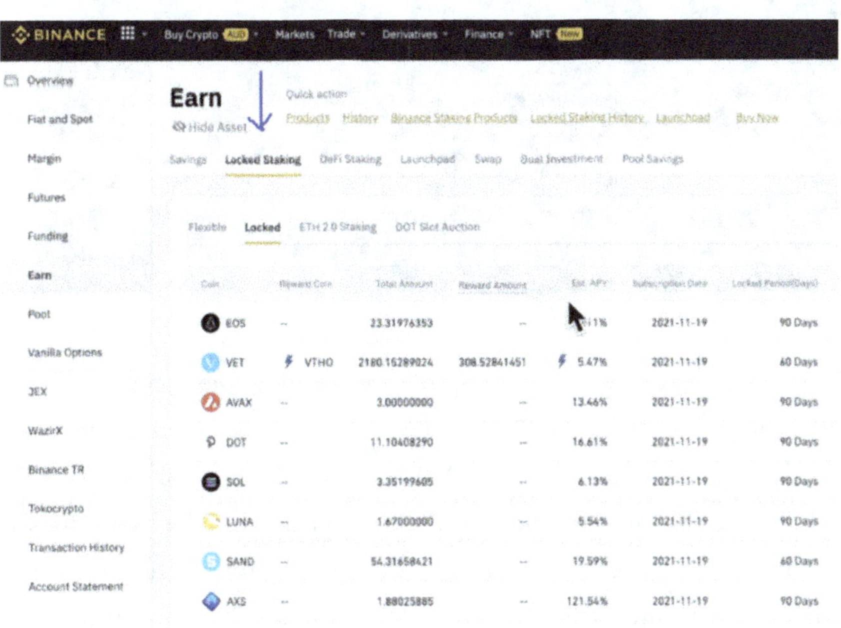

At the same time, I've got some of these cryptos making passive income in the d5 space, particularly in staking and farming. For example, I still have some Enjin coins sitting in the uni swaps liquidity pool and earning trading fees. There are lots of exciting things that you can do.

Below is a bunch of Metaverses-specific cryptocurrencies. They are Axie, Mana, Sand, Enjin, and so forth. Buying and holding these tokens is a direct way of investing in the Metaverse journey.

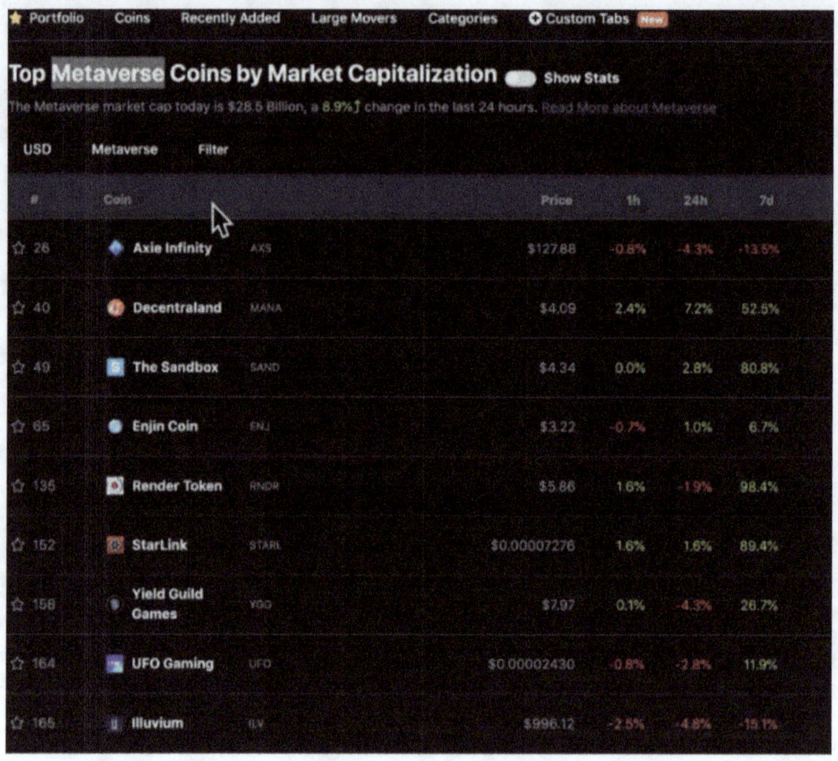

Top Metaverse Coins by Market Capitalization

The Metaverse market cap today is $28.5 Billion, a 8.9% change in the last 24 hours. Read More about Metaverse

#	Coin		Price	1h	24h	7d
28	Axie Infinity	AXS	$127.88	-0.8%	-4.3%	-13.5%
40	Decentraland	MANA	$4.09	2.4%	7.2%	52.5%
49	The Sandbox	SAND	$4.34	0.0%	2.8%	80.8%
65	Enjin Coin	ENJ	$3.22	-0.7%	1.0%	6.7%
135	Render Token	RNDR	$5.86	1.6%	-1.9%	98.4%
152	StarLink	STARL	$0.00007276	1.6%	1.6%	89.4%
158	Yield Guild Games	YGG	$7.97	0.1%	-4.3%	26.7%
164	UFO Gaming	UFO	$0.00002430	-0.8%	-2.8%	11.9%
165	Illuvium	ILV	$996.12	-2.5%	-4.8%	-15.1%

Blockchains and crypto are one approach to building the Metaverse. Don't forget that all other companies are away from the blockchain and doing their part, including big tech ones. We're talking about a 100 trillion dollar stock market. The obvious choice is the Meta platforms. The tech giant was formerly known as Facebook had already made significant investments in virtual reality before their rebranding, including the 2014 acquisition of a VR company Oculus. Mark Zuckerberg, having worked out on Facebook rebranding, is super bullish for the Metaverse. He believes he could replace the internet as we know.

CHAPTER 7: WHAT IS VIRTUAL REALITY

Virtual means not physical, and it means experiencing things, living life via our computers that do not exist. It is simply experiencing a world that is not real. If you saw an image of some paintings that date back to the war era and you begin to visualize yourself having a feel of those paintings, you probably experience the sounds of the guns shooting into the air and so on. It is also the same for music; if you listen to classical or instrumental music with your eyes shut and you begin to dream about things, that's some virtual reality. What about imagining the events that took place in a movie or a book? It seems like it is some form of virtual reality. But it isn't. When you read books, watch a movie, or imagine the events around a painting, it only remains in your thoughts or head; you don't get to feel it or get involved in the activities in the book.

Virtual reality is an interactive 3D world created by the computer that you can experience and explore to the extent that you feel everything there physically and mentally. In virtual worlds, you have to believe that you are in a different world, and you must keep believing that, or the representation of this virtual reality will fade off. You also have to be very interactive; the

VR world moves everywhere with you as you go about. You can read a book and be transported to the sea without having a true experience of being transported, which is not interactive enough. A virtual world has to be very large and filled with details so you can have lots of things to explore. And it should be engaging. It should be very interactive and believable, and it should engage your body and mind. War artists' paintings can give us a view of what conflict is like, but they cannot deliver the sound, sight, taste, smell, and how it is like to be involved on the battlefield. You can play a VR game that will make you lost in the feel of a warm, so real, and interactive experience for about two hours.

Virtual reality is different. It gives you this illusion that you are living in the world; it is interactive; as you respond to the things you see and touch, they will also respond to you change your direction to another place what you will see or hear will change to match the new perspective.

What Is Virtual Reality?

Virtual reality headsets erase your view, bringing the illusion of being elsewhere. When worn, virtual reality headsets like the HTC Vive Cosmos, PlayStation VR, Oculus Quest, Valve Index, and others are opaque and hide off your environment. You might assume you're blindfolded if you put them on when they're off.

However, when you turn on the headsets, the lens refracts the LCD or OLED displays inside, filling one's field of view with whatever is displayed. Examples are a 360-degree film, a game, or the virtual environment created by the platform's user interfaces. The helmet transports you to wherever it wants you to go, eclipsing the natural world in favor of a virtual one.

You have tethered VR headsets like the Play Station VR, and standalone VR headsets like Quest 2 utilize six-degrees-of-freedom (6DOF) motion tracking. This technology is provided through sensors or cameras, outward-facing cameras (for the Quest 2) or (for the Index and PS VR). This implies that the headsets detect the direction you're facing and any movement you make in those directions. With 6DOF motion controllers, you can move about in a virtual area with virtual hands. Although this area is usually only a few square meters, it is more immersive than simply standing stationary and staring in different directions. The disadvantage is that you must be cautious not to trip over any cables connecting the headset to your computer or gaming system.

Types of Virtual Reality

There are so many types of virtual reality. Virtual reality is often used as a marketing word for introducing interactive video games, television programs, and 3D movies. But none of them can be said to be a virtual reality as they don't fully immerse you as a partial or fully virtual world. It is not all the virtual reality that will give you the experience that you need.

The Fully Immersive Virtual World

Suppose you want to enjoy a total virtual reality experience. In that case, you should have a gadget that you can use to enjoy this complex virtual world, and the computer should be able to detect anything that is going on and even adjust to your experience each time. The hardware linked to your computer must fully immerse you into the virtual world as you move around. If you truly want to enjoy these virtual realities, you will need a head-mounted display with stereo sound and two screens. You will like to wear one or two sensory gloves. You can also move about in the room, with a loudspeaker around you so the images can be projected from the outer side.

The Web-Based Virtual Reality

Some virtual reality games are available on the web. But most people would rather search for ways to play virtual reality games rather than the virtual reality that can be played on the web.

Non-Immersive

Non-immersive virtual reality might include an incredibly realistic flight simulator on a home PC, mostly if it has headphones, a big screen, or surround sound, and a real joystick and other controls. Not everyone wants or needs to be wholly absorbed in a different world. An architect might create a detailed 3D model of a new building that can be explored with a mouse on a desktop computer to demonstrate to clients. Even if it doesn't immerse you, a lot of people would consider that a form of virtual reality. Computer archaeologists frequently produce intriguing reconstructions for 3D of long-lost settlements that you can roam around and explore in the same way. They don't transport you hundreds or thousands of years back in time or recreate prehistoric noises, scents, or tastes. Still, they provide more immersive know-how than a few pastel drawings or even an animated film.

Collaborative

What of games in a "virtual environment," such as Second Life and Minecraft? Do they fall within the category of VR? They match the first four of our requirements (believable, interactive, computer-generated, and explorable), but not fifth: they don't completely immerse you. However, they do provide something that cutting-edge VR often does not: collaboration: the concept of sharing a virtual world experience with others, frequently in real-time or near to it. Collaboration and sharing are likely to become more essential aspects of virtual reality in the future.

Virtual Reality Devices

This section provides a brief review of the main VR devices on the market.

Oculus Rift CV1

After having produced two models aimed at software developers, called DK1 and DK2 (Developer Kit), Oculus releases the first version intended for the consumer market of the Oculus Rift.

Technical features: The viewer uses a dual-display system, with 1200×1080 pixel resolution, an optical tracking system, and stereo speakers.

The displays, updated to a frequency of 90 Hz, are AMOLED type, a variant of OLED technology commonly used in the production of small displays, such as those found in smartphones. The choice of OLED technology, compared to the less expensive LCD technology, is justified by the much lower response speed of OLED, which allows, through a technique called low persistence or strobing, to reduce motion blur due to the persistence of the image on the retina.

Due to the presence of two separate displays, the distance between the displays can be adjusted through a mechanical system.

Tracking system: The tracking system, called Constellation Tracking System, is optical and uses two sensors that can detect the position of the infrared LEDs covering the viewer. From these values, the tracking system determines the position and rotation of the viewer, in relation to the sensor. This is an example of an outside-in tracking system, where the sensors are external.

Oculus Rift S

In 2019, Oculus released a new version of the Rift on the market, called Rift S. Unlike the previous version, the new visor has a single LCD screen with 2560×1440 pixel resolution and a refresh rate of 80 Hz.

In addition to the new display, Rift S also boasts a new inside-out tracking system, called Oculus Insight. Using five cameras placed on the viewer, Rift S is able to track its position and rotation in relation to the surrounding environment, and it is also able to track the infrared LEDs of the controllers.

Oculus Quest

Since 2016, Oculus has announced interest in standalone devices, with the stated goal of entering directly into the mobile end of the VR market. In 2018, the Oculus Go visor is first released, followed in 2019 by the Oculus Quest.

Specifications: Based on the Qualcomm Snapdragon 835 chip, the Oculus Quest is a standalone device that offers a six-degree-of-freedom tracking system (position and rotation), motion controller, OLED display with 1440×1600 resolution and 72 Hz refresh rate.

HTC Vive

The HTC Vive is the result of research carried out by Valve in the field of VR, the result of collaboration between the Taiwanese company HTC and the American developer Valve.

Technical characteristics: The characteristics of the visor are largely equal to those of the Oculus Rift CV1: the visor sports a dual AMOLED screen with a resolution of 1200×1080 pixels and refresh rate at 90 Hz, a field of view of about 110 ° (measured along the diagonal). The main difference is the tracking system, called Lighthouse, which allows the device to support a 360-degree tracking mode in a volume of a few square meters, called room-scale.

Tracking system: The Lighthouse tracking system, developed by Valve, makes use of base stations that generate laser beams; photoreceptor sensors, scattered on the viewer and controllers (or, more generally, on the object to be tracked), detect their position in space, allowing to determine the position and rotation of the tracked object.

Samsung Gear VR

In 2015, Samsung released the Samsung Gear VR, produced in collaboration with Oculus, as an accessory for its line of high-end smartphones.

The Samsung Gear VR can be seen as a much more advanced version of Google Cardboard, as it is a container in which you can place your Samsung smartphone, which will act as a display and processing unit.

Application Areas

Entertainment and Culture

In recent years, thanks mainly to the new wave of commercial visors started by Oculus Rift, interest in virtual reality has been rekindled in the general public, particularly in gaming and more generally in entertainment. In addition, other activities and areas that are by nature more education-oriented, have opened up to the novelty of VR to try to attract the younger audience, usually more attentive to technological innovations; thus we can find virtual museums and theme parks, interactive theatrical performances and more.

The main driver that unites these new experiences is the sense of immersion and involvement of the public, which is no longer a passive part but can have if desired, an active role. The direct interaction that new virtual and augmented reality technologies allow becomes a means to communicate information in new and interesting ways.

Education

Living in a technological society, younger generations are familiar with the use of all forms of technology, growing up, from childhood, in contact with more or less advanced technological devices. Unlike adults, who tend to be timider in the face of technology, young people show much less hesitation in trying out the latest innovations they hear about through advertising or word of mouth. In recent years, schools, in all its different levels from kindergarten to university, have begun to include VR and AR in their teaching processes in order to improve educational offerings.

Architecture

When buying a house, redoing the kitchen or the bathroom, or more generally when renovating a house, it is becoming increasingly common for the client to have the opportunity to see in advance the final result of the work, faithfully reconstructed in 3D, sometimes even in immersive mode, *i.e.* using a Virtual Reality helmet.

This practice, called architectural visualization, allows not only the client to evaluate the result, but also the architect to verify the validity of his project. In addition, since virtual reconstruction is much less expensive and time-consuming, it is possible to make changes, even frequent ones, to the original project; by evaluating different factors and aspects of the project before the actual construction, design errors are greatly reduced.

Production and Marketing

In the manufacturing phase of a product, processes based on new technologies such as virtual reality can replace traditional processes that are deemed more expensive, unsafe, and inefficient.

For example, before a product reaches its final form, it undergoes a series of changes, evolving from its initial idea to become the product you find on the shelves of your local store. The prototyping process can be extremely costly and time-consuming, though necessary to achieve the quality standards required by the customer. In all, VR can be a very cost-effective and time-saving solution for prototyping, which is why it is gradually replacing the traditional prototyping process wherever possible.

Military

In the military field, virtual reality is used as a tool for training; it is particularly useful for training soldiers to deal appropriately with conflict scenarios and unusual and dangerous situations, without running the risk of being seriously injured or dying.

Compared to traditional training methods, VR simulation is less expensive and does not put soldiers' safety at risk. Devices commonly used by soldiers in training sessions are head-mounted displays and data gloves, both of which are tracked to allow interaction with virtual objects.

Examples of Virtual Reality

Some examples of augmented reality applications:

Timberland

Timberland, using Kinect motion detection technology in connection with augmented reality: the virtual dressing room allows people to see an image of their face on a model's body (similar in size and characteristics to the user in front of the screen/mirror) and to try on clothes and accessories, combinations of styles, staying in front of the screen (even outside the store) then continuing the in-store shopping, bringing into the dressing room only clothes and accessories that have already received positive opinions.

Bayern Munich

The Bavarian company has created an app to take selfies with favorite players without going as far as Munich. It has been specially designed for those who cannot physically follow their team (e.g fans abroad) or are simply not regular stadium fans. Considering that the pandemic has emptied the stadiums this could have a very interesting development in the future.

Land Rover

Land Rover has developed an interesting example of AR. It is called "Transparent Bonnet" and provides the driver with an experience unthinkable until a few years ago: it creates an effective transparent view of the ground below through the bonnet, revolutionizing the driver's visibility. Think about how many motor lovers would like to live this experience.

Gatwick Airport

An app has been developed for passengers transiting from Gatwick Airport (a solution that has won several international awards and recognition precisely for the effective use of new technologies that bring benefits to people.

With over 2,000 beacons in the two terminals, travelers can use some maps characterized by AR (through indications and signals transmitted to the mobile phone) to move more easily inside the airport.

Figment AR

Viro Media's "Figment AR" application creates interactive, immersive, and above all amusing scenes, transforming the place where children find themselves into a world to be completely explored; the first thought obviously goes to the exploration of past historical eras, thinking of studying prehistory, the ancient Romans or the medieval age with the user dropped to perfection in the epoch to be studied.